P9-EEM-456

Lucy

Lucy

TIM FREW

Photographs from the

HOWARD FRANK ARCHIVES/PERSONALITY PHOTOS

BARNES
&NOBLE
BOOKS
NEW YORK

This edition published by Barnes & Noble, Inc.
by arrangement with Michael Friedman Publishing Group, Inc.

1998 Barnes & Noble Books

©1996 by Michael Friedman Publishing Group, Inc.

All rights reserved. No part of this publication may be reproduced,
stored in a retrieval system, or transmitted, in any form or by any
means, electronic, mechanical, photocopying, recording, or otherwise,
without prior written permission from the publisher.

ISBN 0-7607-1080-5

M 10 9 8 7 6 5 4 3 2 1

Editor: Sharyn Rosart
Art Director: Lynne Yeamans
Designer: Susan E. Livingston
Photography Editor: Christopher C. Bain

Photographs from the Howard/Frank Archives/Personality Photos, Inc.
P.O. Box 50
Midwood Station
Brooklyn, NY 11230

Printed in China by Leefung-Asco Printers Ltd.
Color separations by HBM Print Ltd.

Dedication

To my niece Dorothy, one of the biggest Lucy fans I know.

CONTENTS

Introduction

Above: Partners not only in marriage, Lucille and Desi cofounded Desilu Productions, which became one of Hollywood's most successful production companies.

Opposite: This 1940s publicity photograph captures a glamorous, sophisticated Lucille, an image quite unlike the madcap comedienne she would later become famous for.

Left: Lucille on the set of *I Love Lucy* with Vivian Vance and Bill Frawley.

Right: Gale Gordon and Lucille first worked together on her radio show, *My Favorite Husband*, in 1949, when Gordon joined the cast as a regular. He played her husband's boss.

On September 8, 1951, an eager crowd filed through a door under a sign proclaiming "The Desilu Playhouse." The "playhouse" was actually the converted Stage 2 of the General Service Studios at 1040 North Las Palmas Avenue, Hollywood, California. Once the site of the filming of such classics as the Marx Brothers' *Night in Casablanca*, Harold Lloyd's *Safety Last*, and Howard Hughes' *Hell's Angels*, General Service had fallen on hard times. In an attempt to raise enough cash to placate creditors, General Service had rented Stage 2 to the upstart Desilu Productions to film a series for the relatively new medium of television. "Desilu" was an amalgamation of the names Desi Arnaz and Lucille Ball; the series was *I Love Lucy*.

Desi's band, under the direction of Wilbur Hatch, played Latin music as audience members took their seats on metal bleachers. A few minutes before filming was to begin, Desi grabbed a mike and started for center stage to warm up the audience. Luckily, a crew member noticed that the fly on Desi's tuxedo was open. So nervous was Desi that he couldn't unjam the zipper and was only able to go onstage after the crew member lent a helping hand.

Once in front of the audience, Arnaz was all smiles. He showed the audience the lights and the moving cameras and promised that the complicated machinery would not block their view. Far from being worried about sightlines, the audience was fascinated with the way a television show was filmed. (The three-camera setup and the overhead flat lighting system—designed by master cinematographer Karl Freund—were new techniques that would revolutionize the live filming of sitcoms for years to come.)

Desi then introduced the cast: William Frawley, whom many in the audience recognized from his work as a character actor; Vivian Vance, who got a nice hand even though she was a virtual unknown; and then, finally, the woman whose name would soon become synonymous with television comedy: "And now the star of the show, the mother of my child, the vice president of Desilu Productions—I'm the president—my favorite redhead, Lucille Ball!"

Lucille came out to a rousing ovation, took a bow, and then introduced her mother, DeDe, who was sitting in the back of the bleachers. The star then sat down in the living room set, picked up a book titled *The Mockingbird Murder Mystery*, and assumed the persona of a woman who would become the most beloved housewife in television history: Lucy Ricardo.

This first *I Love Lucy* episode ever filmed was called "Lucy Thinks Ricky Is Trying to Murder Her." It was not, however, the first episode

to air on television. Due to technical complications in the editing of Episode #1 (a new editing machine, dubbed "the three-headed monster," had to be invented to cut the show), the second Lucy segment, "The Girls Want to Go to a Nightclub," was actually the first show that aired.

Few, if any, people in the audience that night realized that they were about to witness television history in the making. The *I Love Lucy* show would chronicle the misadventures of Lucy and Ricky Ricardo and Fred and Ethel Mertz for nearly ten years and 193 episodes, and would continue to delight television viewers for decades to come in reruns.

Initially, critics were skeptical of the show, but there was no denying the public's unbridled love for Lucy's zany antics. After just two months of episodes, more than 15 million people—one in nine Americans—tuned to CBS for *I Love Lucy* every Monday night. By the end of the first season, that number had more than doubled to 31 million viewers, and the show bumped out *Arthur Godfrey's Talent Scouts* as the most watched show on television.

That same season, Lucille Ball was nominated for an Emmy Award as best comedy performer. The comedian Red Skelton won, but when he reached the podium he declared, "Ladies and gentle-

men, you've given this to the wrong redhead. I don't deserve this. It should go to Lucille Ball." Lucille and the show went on to win Emmys the following year.

Lucille Ball had finally made it. She had become so successful that nothing could stop her: not pregnancy (the writers simply wrote it into the show, despite apprehensions from the sponsor and the network); not an investigation by the House Un-American Activities Committee (the investigation turned out to be more of a public relations nightmare for HUAC than for Lucille); not even a troubled marriage or eventual divorce from Desi (she took over Desilu and went from married housewife to widowed housewife in her subsequent TV series). Yet success had not come easily for Lucille Ball. She was already forty years old and had struggled to make it in the movie business for eighteen years before she filmed that first episode of *I Love Lucy*.

Born in Jamestown, New York, on August 6, 1911, to Desirée (DeDe) and Henry (Had) Ball, Lucille felt the desire to become an actress from an early age. At fifteen, she quit high school and moved to New York City to enroll in the Robert Minton–John Murray Anderson School of Drama, whose star pupil at the time was a strikingly self-confident actress from New England named Bette

Davis. Drama school did not work out for Lucille, however, and after a brief time at the school, John Murray Anderson told Lucille she was wasting her money.

For the next several years Lucille shuttled back and forth between Jamestown and New York City, working on and off as a model for dress designer Hattie Carnegie. Lucille got her first break when she signed on as one of the Goldwyn Girls for an Eddie Cantor musical called *Roman Scandals*. While the job offered her neither fame nor security, it did give her a ticket to Hollywood.

Lucille went from Goldwyn Girl to contract player for Columbia and eventually to RKO, where she appeared in thirty-one movies between 1935 and 1942. While most of these were B movies, Lucille did work her way up from bit player to lead actress and eventually showed a strong talent for comedy. The highlights of her RKO career included *Stage Door*, in which she costarred with Katharine Hepburn and Ginger Rogers; *Room Service*, with the Marx Brothers; and *Too Many Girls*, during the filming of which she met and eventually married a young Cuban entertainer named Desi Arnaz. By the end of her days at RKO she had honed her abilities and was pulling in a large salary; unfortunately, however, her movies were not very successful and stardom eluded her.

In 1942, RKO sold her contract to MGM, where her first film was a Cole Porter musical called *DuBarry Was a Lady*. For this role, Lucille's hair was dyed an intensely bright red, thus giving birth to the "Lucille Ball look." While Lucille's career plugged along at MGM, her fame never lived up to her talent and soon the studio began to doubt that she could ever become a major star.

After all but giving up on the movies, in 1948 Lucille turned to radio, and finally had a hit. The show, called *My Favorite Husband*, starred Lucille as Liz Cooper, a ditsy wife with a habit of getting into scrapes. From radio, it was but a short step to television, although at first Lucille was reluctant to enter the new medium. Part of Lucille's reason for moving to television was to try to save her marriage. Desi's incessant touring with his nightclub act—and the drinking and womanizing that went along with it—had put an immense strain on the Arnaz marriage. CBS was eager to do a series with Lucille based on *My Favorite Husband*, but wanted no part of her Cuban bandleader husband. Lucille, on the other hand, refused to do any series that did not include Desi. Lucille and Desi formed

Far left: Originally brunette, Lucille's hair color changed often during her years as a film actress. The redhead look was born in 1942, and Lucille stayed with it for the rest of her life.

Left: *You Can't Fool Your Wife* (1940), costarring James Ellison, was Lucille's forty-ninth film. She was twenty-nine years old, and stardom continued to elude her.

Desilu Productions to do the series, and then pushed both CBS and the show's sponsor, Phillip Morris, into letting the Arnazes do the show exactly the way they wanted. Both the network and the sponsor reluctantly went along with the persistent couple and were rewarded with the most popular show in television history.

In subsequent series, Lucy Ricardo became Lucy Carmichael and then Lucy Carter, but the character remained essentially the same—a well-meaning, if bumbling, American housewife and mother, whose schemes put her in the most awkward of situations. Lucille Ball's humor was always clean, always physical, and always empathetic. She was a tireless performer and perfectionist who would work with a prop as simple as a paper bag for hours on end until she was able to get it to pop in just the right way. Later in her career, Lucille often exasperated guest stars, many of them entertainment legends in their own right, by pushing them around the set and chiding them for their poor timing and inadequate delivery. She even tallied up the number of laughs co-star Richard Burton "lost" by saying a line the wrong way during rehearsals.

Lucille Ball lived to perform, and in her performing she made millions of people laugh. Blessed with an expressive face, a distinctive voice, and impeccable timing, Lucille was not afraid to look the fool; in fact, she reveled in it. She would stuff her face full of chocolates, roll around in a vat of crushed grapes, blacken her teeth into a hideous grin, and don any manner of absurd costume in order to surprise and delight her audience. This tireless entertainer made seventy-three movies, appeared in fifty-one television specials, and starred in four television series during a career that lasted more than fifty years.

In March 1989, Lucille Ball appeared with Bob Hope at the Oscar ceremony. Lucille had always feared looking old. On *The Lucy Show*, she pressed lighting and makeup people to help hide her wrinkles, and often wore a painful harness under her wig to pull her skin tight. The night of the Oscars, however, she defied her age as she grabbed Hope by the arm and walked onstage wearing a dress with a slit cut practically up to her waist, revealing a taut and youthful-looking leg. The two titans of comedy received a standing ovation from their colleagues that lasted several minutes. Lucille Ball died of a ruptured aorta less than a month later. She can still be seen, however, in all her glory, simply by turning on the television.

Chapter One

Lucy Behind the Scenes

Above: Lucille Desireé Ball was born on Sunday, August 6, 1911. Lucille lived her first three years in Montana and Michigan, where her father worked as a telephone company lineman.

Opposite: Lucille and Desi first met each other in the RKO commissary in 1940. Lucy was filming *Dance, Girl, Dance* and Desi had just arrived at RKO to be in the film version of *Too Many Girls*, a hit musical he had appeared in on Broadway. Lucille was 28 years old, Desi 23.

Right: With his bongo drum, his charisma, and his dark, Latin good looks, Desi Arnaz rode the Latin music craze to a successful nightclub career.

Far right: As a teenager, Lucille had an on-again, off-again modeling career in New York City. At 5 feet, seven inches tall (167.5cm), Lucille had the right look for modelling; ultimately, this led to her opportunity to get into films.

Above: A three-year-old Lucille Ball clutches a favorite doll. After her father's death in 1915, Lucille and her mother moved back to Jamestown, New York.

Right: Desiderio Alberto Arnaz y de Acha III at home in the historic city of Santiago de Cuba. Desi was born to a wealthy Cuban family—his father was mayor of Santiago, his uncle the chief of police.

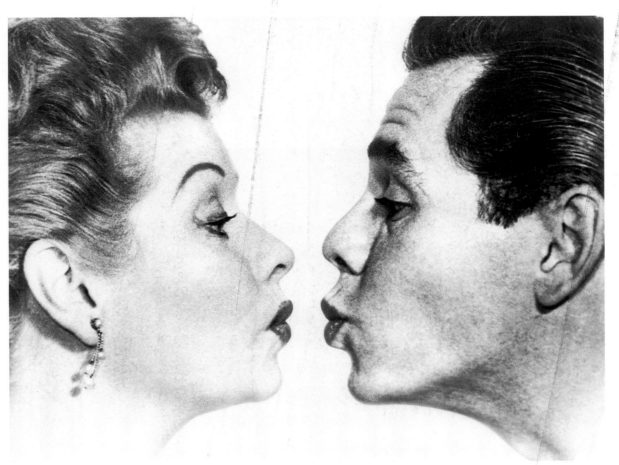

Left: Although Desi was engaged to a dancer named Renée de Marco, and Lucille was involved in a relationship with film director Al Hall (*Here Comes Mr. Jordan*, 1941), Lucille and Desi immediately became caught up in a passionate romance. They were married on November 30, 1940 in Greenwich, Connecticut, less than a year after they met.

Above: Lucille was a bit of a homebody, but Desi loved the night life. Soon after the marriage, Lucille abandoned her rule of staying home on weeknights and began accompanying her husband to restaurants and nightclubs. Here, the two are enjoying the show at the Stork Club.

Desi Arnaz was drafted into the army in 1943, soon after he became a U.S. citizen. Desi and Lucille's relationship was stormy, and the war years were characterized by ferocious quarrels followed by passionate reconciliations.

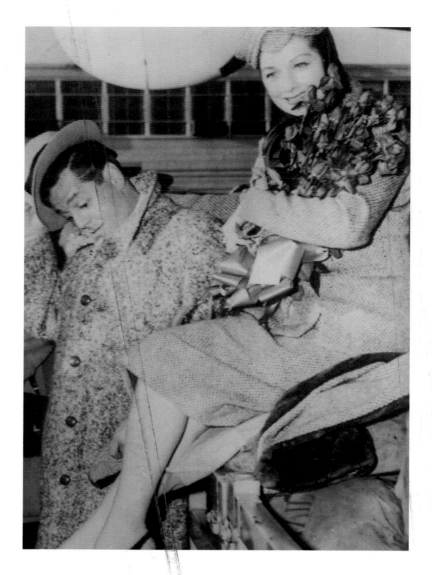

Above: Desi admires Lucille's legs and then lifts her from her perch as they clown around for fans and the press upon their arrival in New York City in February 1948.

Left: Both Lucille and Desi were very close to their mothers. Here is Lucille with her mother, DeDe, and Desi with his mother, Lolita.

Lucille Ball and Desi Arnaz were married for a second time on June 19, 1949, even though their first marriage was still intact. Desi's mother, Lolita, believed the two could not conceive a child because they had not been married in a Catholic ceremony. Six months after the second ceremony, Lucille did conceive, but she soon had a miscarriage.

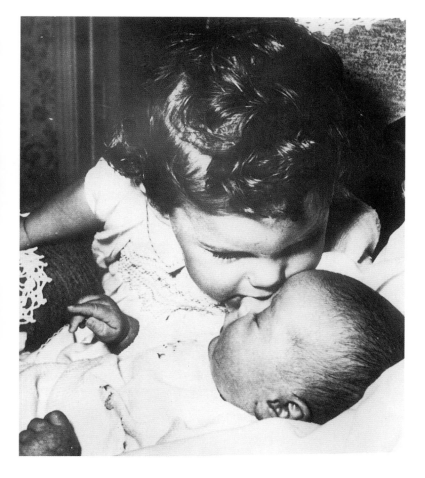

Left: In this picture taken by Desi Sr., eighteen-month-old Lucie welcomes her newborn brother into the family. Since Lucille gave birth via a scheduled cesarean section, the show's writers were able to plan Little Ricky's birth for the same day as Desi Jr.'s.

Below: Ten months after she gave birth to Lucie, Lucille found out she was pregnant again. By this time, *I Love Lucy* was already the number one show on television, and rather than suspend the show, the producers and writers decided to make the character of Lucy Ricardo pregnant as well. Here, Lucille and Desi pose with Desi IV after his christening.

Opposite: On July 17, 1951, just three weeks before her fortieth birthday, Lucille Ball gave birth to a healthy baby girl. Lucille and Desi had chosen the name "Susan" in the event the baby was a girl, but while Lucille recovered from her cesarean section, Desi decided to surprise her, and signed the birth certificate, giving the child the name "Lucie."

Left: Lucille and her mother, DeDe, busy decorating at the Arnaz/Ball ranch in Chatsworth in the San Fernando Valley. Clearly the two share a love for vibrant prints.

Below: In 1955, a kidnapping threat seriously disrupted life at Chatsworth. Lucille and Desi decided to move their family to Beverly Hills, which was closer to the studio.

Opposite: The fact that Lucy Ricardo was a simple yet wacky housewife played a major part in the success of *I Love Lucy*. These publicity photos of Lucille doing chores around the house in Chatsworth were meant to cultivate the actress' image as a housewife. Publicity aside, Lucille very much loved spending her free time at home and took special pride in modest possessions.

Right: After years of strife, Lucille and Desi divorced in 1960. Two years later, Lucille bought out Desi's shares in Desilu Productions. Here Lucille presides over the board of directors. After *I Love Lucy*, Desilu remained one of the premier television production companies through the 1960s, responsible for such ground-breaking shows as *Mission Impossible* and *Star Trek*.

STATEMENT OF TRANSFER OR CHANGE OF NAME
I last registered under the name of

I last registered at and removed from .... Street

.... Precinct

I hereby authorize the cancellation of said registration.

ORIGINAL

Los Angeles City Precinct No. ....

STATE OF CALIFORNIA,
COUNTY OF LOS ANGELES, } ss.

AFFIDAVIT OF REGISTRATION.

The undersigned affiant, being duly sworn, says: I will be at least twenty-one years of age at the time of the next succeeding election, a citizen of the United States ninety days prior thereto, and a resident of the State one year, of the County ninety days, and of the Precinct forty days next preceding such election, and will be an elector of this County at the next succeeding election.

1. I have not registered from any other precinct in the State since January 1, 1936.
(If applicant has so previously registered, mark out the word "not" and fill out the appropriate blanks at the top of the affidavit.)

2. My full name is *Miss Lucile D. Ball*
(Including Christian or given name, and middle name or initial, and in the case of women, the prefix Miss or Mrs.)

3. My residence is *1344 - North Ogden Drive*, ... Side
(Name street or road. If remote from both, then give Sec., Twp., and Range.)

between *Fountain* and *Delongpre* Streets, ... Floor, Room ....

Post-office address at *1344 - North Ogden Drive*

My occupation is *actress*

My height is *5* feet *6½* inches.

I was born in *New York*
(State or Country)
(If a native born citizen you need not answer question No. 7.)

I acquired citizenship by } ....

9. I intend to affiliate at the ensuing primary election with the *Communist* Party.
(If affiliation is not given, write or stamp "Declines to State.")

8. I can .... read the Constitution in the English language; I can .... write my name; I am entitled to vote by reason of having been on October 10, 1911

Miss Lucille D. Ball
(Affiant sign here.)
1344 N. Ogden Dr
(Street Address)

Subscribed and sworn to before me this *19th* day of *March* 193*6*

N° 847584

W. M. KERR, Registrar of Voters,

By ....
Deputy Registrar of Voters.

CANCELLED
BY REASON OF NOT HAVING VOTED AT EITHER THE AUGUST PRIMARY OR ELECTION 1938
W. M. KERR, Register of Voters

Above: In February 1952, members of the House Un-American Activities Committee (HUAC) uncovered this document showing that Lucille Ball had registered as a member of the Communist party in 1936. At first they accepted her explanation that she only joined to please her eccentric grandfather and that she never voted as a Communist, but the committee decided to reopen the case eighteen months later to capitalize on Lucille's popularity. Again she was cleared and her fans still embraced her.

Name placards visible: FRED BALL, JERRY THORPE, W. ARGYLE NELSON

Left: After her marriage ended, Lucille immediately agreed to make a movie with her friend Bob Hope. Desi made a surprise appearance at the luncheon announcing Lucille's return to movies in *The Facts of Life*, which was her first film in five years. Despite their divorce, Lucille and Desi remained friendly. When Lucille suffered a serious fall on the set of *The Facts of Life*, Desi rushed to her side, sparking rumors of reconciliation.

Left: In 1960 Lucille decided to do a Broadway show. *Wildcat* was the story of a woman in the Texas oil fields. While Lucille's return to the stage was welcomed by her fans, critics panned the musical, which closed after a few months. Here, Lucille gets a congratulatory hug from Vivian Vance backstage at the opening night of *Wildcat*.

Right: On November 19, 1961, Lucille Ball married a struggling comedian named Gary Morton. The two had met in New York City, just before the opening of *Wildcat*.

Lucille and Gary wave to fans after their marriage at the Marble Collegiate Church in New York. Gary had signed a prenuptial agreement to stifle rumors that he was nothing but a golddigger.

Chapter Two

Lucy in the Movies

Above: In 1942, Lucille starred with Henry Fonda in *The Big Street*, based on a Damon Runyon short story. Lucille plays a heartless, self-absorbed actress who is paralyzed when her lover pushes her down a set of stairs.

Opposite: Before she became a television star, Lucille was part of Hollywood's studio system; by 1951 she had appeared in some sixty-five movies.

When the mother of one of the Goldwyn Girls refused to let her daughter go to Hollywood, Lucille Ball got her first break. Here, the Goldwyn Girls line up for a publicity shot for *Roman Scandals*, Lucille Ball's first motion picture. Can you pick her out of the lineup?

ight: Lucille Ball pictured with William Cagney, brother of James Cagney, at Hollywood's famed Brown Derby in 1933. The photograph was originally labeled "One of the Newest Hollywood Romances." William was under contract with RKO at the time.

elow: It was the Blondes vs. the Brunettes, two teams of Goldwyn Girls, in a comic polo match benefiting the Marion Davies Foundation on May 13, 1934. Many years before she began dyeing her hair red, Lucille Ball posed with her "blonde" teammates. From left to right: Vivian Keefer (bending over), Barbara Pepper, Lucille Ball, and Jane Hamilton.

In 1934, Lucille left her job as a Goldwyn Girl, worked a brief stint as a contract actress for Columbia, and then signed on with RKO for a salary of $75 per week. RKO released this publicity shot of their up-and-coming young starlets for 1935. From left to right: Lucille Ball, Margaret Callahan, Joan Hodges, Anne Shirley, Phyllis Brooks, and Molly Lamont.

Above: Lucille's first film for RKO was the musical *Roberta* (1935), in which she played a model. The film starred Irene Dunne and featured the new dance team of Fred Astaire and Ginger Rogers.

Right: Lela Rogers (who was Ginger Rogers' mother) ran a workshop for young RKO contract players on the RKO lot. She would stage plays with the RKO hopefuls and charge a quarter for admission. Here, Lucille Ball acts in the short play "Breakfast for Vanora."

Right: Lucille Ball and Jack Oakie in a scene from *Annabel Takes a Tour* (1938), the second of two "Annabel" comedies (the first was *The Affairs of Annabel*) that Lucille made for RKO. Although these B movies had limited success, they showcased Lucille's early abilities at physical comedy. The "Annabel" movies chronicled the adventures of an actress whose zany publicity stunts get her into trouble.

Left: Lucille's first critically praised film was the acclaimed *Stage Door* (1937), starring Katharine Hepburn, Ginger Rogers (shown here with Lucille), Adolphe Menjou, Andrea Leeds, Eve Arden, and Ann Miller. Eve Arden would later star in *Our Miss Brooks*, a television show filmed at Desilu.

Above: In 1938, Lucille was cast in the Marx Brothers film *Room Service*. (Ann Miller also appeared in the film.) Based on the hit Broadway play of the same name, *Room Service* was one of the Brothers' least successful films. The only Marx Brother that Lucille got along with was Harpo, who many years later made a guest appearance on *I Love Lucy*.

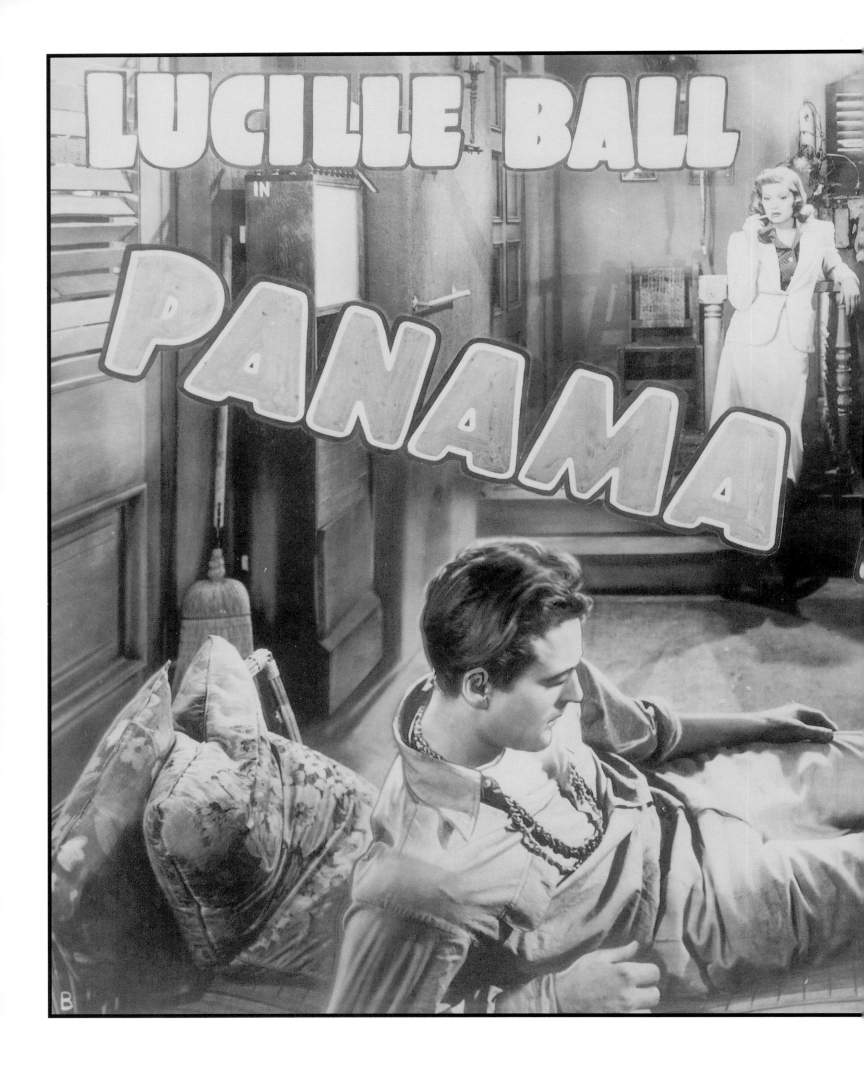

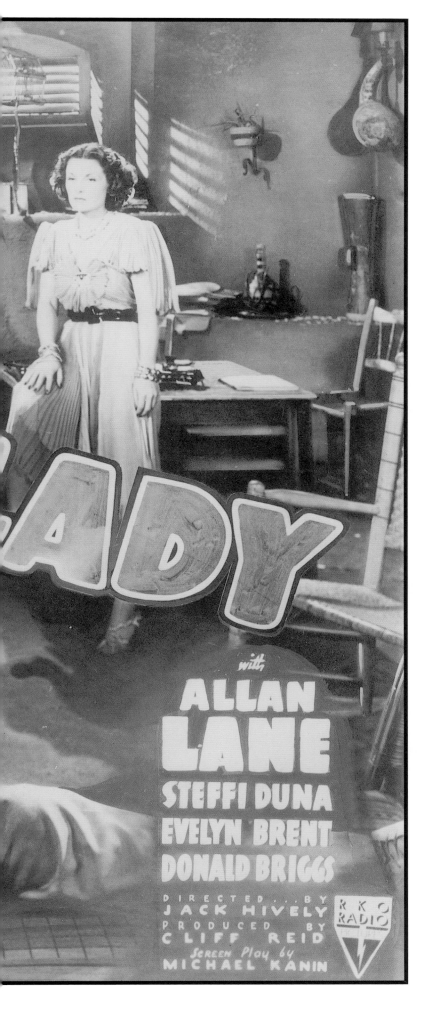

LADY

with

ALLAN LANE
STEFFI DUNA
EVELYN BRENT
DONALD BRIGGS

DIRECTED...BY
JACK HIVELY
PRODUCED BY
CLIFF REID
Screen Play by
MICHAEL KANIN

RKO RADIO

Left: Production was interrupted several times during the 1939 film *Panama Lady* because Lucille fell ill from exhaustion. The movie, in which Lucille played a dancer stranded in Central America, costarred Allan Lane. It was universally panned by critics.

Below: Lucille's striking coloring—pale white skin, blue eyes, and bright red hair—served to distinguish her from other starlets of the period.

Right: In her twenty-third RKO film, *You Can't Fool Your Wife* (1940), Lucille Ball played a frumpy housewife who impersonates a wild Argentinean thrill-seeker.

Below: Lucille scored her second hit in a row with MGM in 1943 (the first being *DuBarry Was a Lady*), in the comedy *Best Foot Forward*. She played herself making a visit to a military school as a publicity stunt. The film grossed more than $2 million and marked the movie debuts of Nancy Walker and June Allyson.

Above: *Sorrowful Jones* (1949) was the first of only two pictures Lucille made on loan to Paramount. She co-starred with Bob Hope (left) and William Demarest. Ball and Hope would go on to make three more films together, and Hope would appear as a guest star on *I Love Lucy*.

Left: By the time Lucille Ball made a brief appearance as herself in *Abbott and Costello in Hollywood*, MGM had all but given up on making her a major movie star. Threatened with a cut in pay, Lucille left MGM three films later.

Above: In 1949, Lucille played a loyal team secretary in the melodrama *Easy Living*, about a football player at the end of his career. The film costarred Victor Mature, Lizabeth Scott, Sonny Tufts, and Lloyd Nolan.

Left: *Fancy Pants*, a 1950 remake of the 1935 classic *Ruggles of Red Gap*, cast Bob Hope as Lucille's British butler on a trip through the Wild West.

Right: In the second film of her three-picture deal with Columbia, Lucille starred in the slapstick hit *The Fuller Brush Girl* (1950), a spin-off of Red Skelton's successful *Fuller Brush Man*. With physical gags evocative of her later work in *I Love Lucy*, Lucille was finally able to showcase her comedic talents.

R ight: While at the height of their TV popularity, Lucille Ball and Desi Arnaz made *The Long, Long Trailer* (1954), directed by Vincente Minnelli. Despite the runaway success of *I Love Lucy*, MGM was hesitant to make the film, believing that the public would not pay to go see stars they could see on television for free. Starring Lucille and Desi as a newly married couple living in a mobile home, *The Long, Long Trailer* was MGM's most successful film of the year.

ight and below: *Forever Darling* (1956) starred Lucille and Desi as a couple whose troubled marriage is rescued by an angel played by James Mason. Actor Louis Calhern also appeared in the film. MGM gave Desi the opportunity to produce the film. He believed that many of the techniques of television filming could be used in movie-making to bring in a quality film in a shorter period of time. Unfortunately, his money-saving strategies undercut his efforts and the end result was a lower-quality movie that was panned by the critics.

elow: In 1960, Lucille made *The Facts of Life*, a comedy about adultery, with Bob Hope. During the filming of one scene, Lucille fell and was knocked unconscious. Upon awakening, she stared up at an anxious Hope and said, "I hope the ambulance is a Chrysler." Chrysler was Hope's television sponsor.

I n 1968, Lucille made *Yours, Mine, and Ours* with Henry Fonda. The story of a widow with eight children who marries a widower with ten children, it grossed more than $20 million.

Chapter Three

I Love Lucy

Above: Lucille performing her role as housewife Liz Cooper in the radio comedy *My Favorite Husband*, which went on the air in 1948. This popular show served as the inspiration for the *I Love Lucy* television series.

Opposite: Vivian Vance, Lucille Ball, Desi Arnaz, and William Frawley (clockwise from top left) were perhaps the most famous neighbors in television history. Despite their success as a married couple on screen, Vivian Vance and William Frawley never got along during the nine years the show ran.

Below: Exasperated by the protracted negotiations with CBS, in 1951 Lucille and Desi decided to produce the pilot for the *I Love Lucy* television series on their own. Prior to filming the pilot, their characters' names were Larry and Lucy Lopez; Fred and Ethel were not yet written into the concept. Lucille was six months pregnant, and wore loose outfits to disguise her condition.

Above: Lucille performs on an episode of *My Favorite Husband* with Joan Davis. In 1949, Gale Gordon was added to the cast. Gordon would later star as Mr. Mooney in *The Lucy Show* and Harry Carter in *Here's Lucy*.

P rior to the filming of each *I Love Lucy* episode, Desi Arnaz would "warm up" the crowd by telling a few jokes, explaining how the filming worked, and introducing the cast.

"I LOVE LUCY"

Left: It was Desi's idea to use a cartoon logo for the show to fill in the black space before the commercials.

Below: *I Love Lucy* employed many filming and lighting techniques never before used on television. The use of three cameras and overhead flat lighting quickly became the standard for filming a sitcom before a live audience.

Above: Influenced by a murder mystery she is reading, Lucy suspects that Ricky is plotting against her in "Lucy Thinks Ricky Is Trying to Murder Her." Here, she switches the drinks while Ricky's back is turned. Although this was the first episode of *I Love Lucy* to be filmed, it did not air until the fourth week because the editing process took several weeks.

Above: Ethel's misguided attempt at fortune-telling points to Lucy's impending death and convinces her that Ricky truly is trying to kill her. Later in the episode, Lucy overhears Ricky say, "I've decided to get rid of her....I'll probably miss her some, but in a few weeks I can get a new one." Little did she know that Ricky was actually talking about firing a singer.

Below: The original print of "Drafted" included a "surprise" segment with Ethel, Lucy, Ricky, and Fred dressed up in Santa Claus outfits and singing "Jingle Bells." The ninth episode, it first aired on Christmas Eve, 1951.

Above: In "Drafted," Lucy becomes convinced that Ricky has been drafted into the U.S. Army, after she reads a letter from the War Department requesting that Ricky appear at Fort Dix. The request, however, is for Ricky to entertain the troops. When he asks Fred to come along, Ethel thinks Fred has been drafted as well.

Right: In "Pioneer Women" (which first aired on March 31, 1952), Lucy and Ethel try their hands at baking their own bread. When Lucy uses thirteen cakes of yeast instead of three, she get quite a surprise upon opening the oven door. The mammoth bread used in the show was a real loaf of rye baked by the Union Made Bakery.

Left: In "The Freezer," after she and Ethel hide two sides of beef in the unlit furnace—so that Ricky won't find out about a $483 meat bill—Lucy accidentally locks herself inside a huge walk-in freezer, turning herself into a "human popsicle." Fred lights the furnace to help thaw out the frozen Lucy and the meat begins to cook.

In one of the most famous *I Love Lucy* episodes of all, "Lucy Does a TV Commercial," Lucy connives to appear as the "Vitameatavegamin Girl." After several rehearsals and many spoonfuls of the elixir, Lucy becomes hilariously drunk; Vitameatavegamin is 23 percent alcohol.

Below: In "The Handcuffs," Lucy manacles herself to Ricky after seeing Fred perform a magic trick with a set of trick handcuffs. She soon finds out, however, that the handcuffs she used date back to the Civil War and have no key. To complicate matters, Ricky is due to appear on a live television show in just a few hours.

Above: Lucille Ball was never afraid to appear in outlandish costumes or bizarre makeup when taking on the persona of Lucy Ricardo. In "The Operetta," she blackened her teeth when Lucy Ricardo played Camille, queen of the gypsies, in a play for the Wednesday Afternoon Fine Arts League.

Above: In "Job Switching," Lucy and Ethel go to work at a candy factory while Ricky and Fred stay home and do housework. In one of their finest comic moments, Lucy and Ethel stuff chocolates in their mouths in an attempt to keep up with a fast-moving conveyor belt.

Right: Meanwhile, Ricky and Fred fare no better at home, as Ricky ruins the ironing, then destroys the kitchen as he attempts to make *arroz con pollo* for dinner. (In real life, however, Desi Arnaz was an accomplished cook and *arroz con pollo* was one of his specialties.)

ight: The Ricardos give the Mertzes a new television set for their anniversary in "The Courtroom," but when Ricky tries to adjust the set, it blows up. Fred then kicks in the picture tube of the Ricardos' set and the two couples end up in court.

eft: A helpful Desi assists in cleaning up Lucille after filming the candy-making mishap. "Job Switching" began the second season (1952–1953) of *I Love Lucy* and remains one of the all-time favorite episodes among many fans.

ight: Ricky is exasperated as they try to settle on names for the baby in "Pregnant Women Are Unpredictable." Lucy: "I want the names to be unique and euphonious." Ricky: "Okay. Unique if it's a boy and Euphonious if its a girl." Lucille's real-life pregnancy was worked into the show and marked the first time a TV show dealt with pregnancy in a straightforward way.

bove: Lucy gets a taste of early motherhood when Little Ricky won't sleep. The neighbors complain about the crying, and one of them shows Ethel (the landlord) a clause in the lease forbidding children in the building. Even though the tenants threaten to move out, Ethel sticks by her friend and godchild. This was the first episode filmed after Lucille's four months of maternity leave.

Above: Lucy collapses in exhaustion after a futile attempt at selling a vacuum cleaner she was afraid to return. "Sales Resistance," which used a flashback technique, was filmed before Lucille Ball had her baby, but was used after the seven original "baby episodes" in order to give Lucille some time to rest before and after childbirth. In the beginning of the episode, Lucy is in her hospital bed while Ricky, Fred, and Ethel reminisce about her vacuum-cleaner escapades.

Left: After an argument about "Equal Rights," Lucy and Ethel are forced to wash dishes in an Italian restaurant after Ricky and Fred refuse to pay their wives' portion of the bill. This script called for Lucy to blow into and pop a paper bag. Always a perfectionist in her work with props, Lucille practiced popping the bag for three hours, using different-sized and shaped bags.

Right: Tired of being golf widows, Lucy and Ethel decide to take up the game in "The Golf Game," but the boys make up a set of absurd rules to discourage them. The girls, however, get revenge with the help of golf pro Jimmy Demaret.

Right: The night before *I Love Lucy* began its fourth season, Ed Sullivan honored Desi and Lucille by devoting his entire *Toast of the Town* program to "television's most popular couple."

Below: After 109 episodes in New York, the Ricardos and the Mertzes head to Los Angeles in "California, Here We Come." Scheduled to leave at 6 A.M., they spend several hours packing and unpacking the car, until they finally depart at 6 P.M. Here, they sing "California, Here I Come" as they finally cross the George Washington Bridge.

Right: Lucy's tireless attempts to break into show business finally pay off in "Lucy Gets In Pictures"; she lands a role as a showgirl in an MGM musical. Not all goes smoothly, however, as she has trouble with an enormous feathered headdress. The episode harks back to Lucille Ball's days as a Goldwyn Girl and her first film, *Roman Scandals*.

Above: Harpo Marx and "Harpo" Ricardo mug for the camera in the famous episode named after the guest star. In one of the most memorable scenes from *I Love Lucy*, Harpo and Lucy reenact the classic mirror pantomime scene from the Marx Brothers film *Duck Soup*.

Above: "Ricky Sells the Car" for a profit and decides to return to the East Coast via train. But he forgets about the Mertzes, who traveled to California with them in the car. Vivian: "I suppose when he sold the car, the back seat went with it?" Fred buys a used Harley with a sidecar, and the Mertzes are all set to head east...until he backs the bike into a brick wall.

Left: In "Lucy Visits Grauman's," the premiere episode of the show's fifth season (1955–1956), Lucy becomes obsessed with Hollywood souvenirs. Here, she and Ethel try to steal John Wayne's footprints after Lucy notices his concrete "block is loose."

In "The Passports," Lucy may not be able to go to Europe with Ricky because her hometown has no record of her birth, and she can't get a passport without a birth certificate. Lucy threatens to stow away in a steamer trunk and promptly locks herself in.

Right: While in Italy, Lucy gets cast in a movie called *Bitter Grapes*. Thinking the movie is about the Italian winemaking industry, Lucy decides to research her role by dressing in peasant garb and walking to a wine town, where she is immediately put to work as a grape stomper in the episode entitled "Lucy's Italian Movie."

Above: At first Lucy has fun stomping the grapes, but she soon tires of it. When she tries to take a break, she and her partner get into a sloppy fight. Lucy, covered with grape stains, returns to Rome only to learn that the movie has nothing to do with wine, and her role was to be that of a typical American tourist. The director turns her down and gives the role to Ethel.

Left: Fred and Ethel play a two-headed dragon in a dream sequence in "Lucy Goes to Scotland." In Lucy's dream, Scotty MacTavish Mac-Dougal MacCardo (Ricky in a kilt) loses his courage when it comes time to save Lucy from the dragon. Lucy wakes up from her nightmare, hits Ricky with a pillow, and shouts, "You coward!"

Right: Lucy tries to coax milk from a reluctant cow in "Lucy's Bicycle Trip."

Lucy substitutes as a pizza maker for her Italian friend Mario Orsatti, who may get deported if he tries to go back to work in "Visitor from Italy." As the dough, flour, cheese, and sauce fly through the air, Lucille Ball once again shows her genius for physical humor and her uncanny ability to manipulate props.

In "Deep Sea Fishing," the second of several episodes that took place in Florida and Cuba, Lucy & Ethel and Ricky & Fred catch each other sneaking one-hundred-pound (45kg) tunas (both from the fish market) into the Ricardos' bathroom. The reason is a contest of men vs. women: who can catch the bigger fish?

Above: Bob Hope guest-starred in "Lucy and Bob Hope" to lead off the show's sixth season (1956–1957). Lucy dresses as a Cleveland Indians player to try to persuade Hope to appear at Ricky's new nightspot, Club Babalu.

Above: Lucy announces that Superman (George Reeves) will make an appearance at Little Ricky's birthday party. When she finds out that the "Man of Steel" can't make it, Lucy decides to impersonate him in "Lucy and Superman." Here, she climbs out onto the ledge in full superhero garb, getting ready to make her grand entrance.

Above, right: Lucy feels Superman's flexed biceps. A little more than two years after filming this episode, George Reeves, depressed about being typecast as Superman, committed suicide.

Right: Keith Thibodeaux was the child actor who played Little Ricky. In real life Keith was a good friend of Desi Jr. and often stayed with the Arnaz family.

Right: About midway through the sixth season, at the beginning of 1957, the Ricardos and the Mertzes moved to the country (Westport, Connecticut). In "Lucy Raises Chickens," Lucy comes up with an idea for raising a little extra money. She and Ethel, however, buy five hundred chicks before Fred has a chance to finish the chicken coop. Pandemonium ensues when Little Ricky frees the chicks from their temporary home in the Ricardos' den.

Left: Lucy overhears a snippet of conversation and mistakenly thinks that Ethel and her new friend Betty Ramsey (Mary Jane Croft) are going to throw her and Ricky a surprise "Housewarming" party. Lucy practices acting surprised as she waits for the party that never comes.

Above: Lucy examines a poster for Yankee Doodle Day in Westport, Connecticut, where Ricky is scheduled to make a speech unveiling a one-of-a-kind statue of a minuteman in "The Ricardos Dedicate a Statue." Lucy, of course, accidentally destroys the statue—and decides to impersonate it at the ceremony. This was the last of the half-hour *I Love Lucy* episodes. For the show's seventh, eighth, and ninth seasons, a total of thirteen one-hour episodes were filmed.

Above: Milton Berle, Desi Arnaz, and Lucille Ball, three of the most influential people in the history of television, pose in a publicity still for "Milton Berle Hides out at the Ricardos," the first of three episodes to air in the final season (1959–1960) of the *I Love Lucy* show.

Chapter Four

The Later Years

Above: In the 1970s and early 1980s, Lucille made numerous television appearances, hosting specials and making guest appearances on shows hosted by Bob Hope and others. She also made a movie, *Mame*, in 1974.

Opposite: From 1962 to 1968, Lucille starred in *The Lucy Show*. In 1966, Lucille gave one of her best performances on the show when Robert Stack guest-starred as an FBI agent out to arrest a gangster. Here, Lucy impersonates gun moll Barbara Nichols. *The Untouchables*, starring Stack as Eliot Ness, had been one of Desilu's early hit television series.

Below: The musical *Wildcat*, by Cy Coleman (*Sweet Charity*) and N. Richard Nash (*The Rainmaker*), was Lucille's Broadway debut. It opened on December 16, 1960. Despite strong attendance, the show was panned by critics and closed after a few months because of Lucille's poor health.

Opposite: On October 1, 1962, Lucille Ball returned to television with *The Lucy Show*—this time as the widow Lucy Carmichael— and brought her longtime friend and *I Love Lucy* costar, Vivian Vance, along with her to play her divorcée roommate, Vivian Bagley.

Above: One year into the new show, Lucille brought Gale Gordon aboard to play Lucy Carmichael's comic foil, Mr. Mooney, the banker. Lucy had originally wanted Gordon to play the part of Fred Mertz in *I Love Lucy*, but he was locked into another TV role at the time.

Left: Dick Martin (left) played Lucy's airline pilot neighbor who often stopped by to lend a helping hand when needed. Ironically, in 1968, Martin's innovative hit show *Laugh-In* would compete in the same time slot as Lucy, draw higher ratings, and make Lucy's comedy seem somewhat out of touch. In the 1970-1971 seasons, however, *Here's Lucy*, still competing in the same time slot, reclaimed the lead and was number three on television; *Laugh-In* had fallen to thirteenth place.

Above: Lucy and Vivian hang on for dear life as their attempt at do-it-yourself plumbing goes awry. (When installing a new shower, they forgot to put in a drain.) For her new show, Lucille stuck with the same type of comic predicaments that had made *I Love Lucy* such a big hit.

Right: After accidentally getting locked inside the bank vault, Mr. Mooney and Lucy try to pass the time by playing cards. Gordon once described Lucille Ball as "the only genius I ever knew."

Left: The blustery yet lovable Harry Carter was forever falling victim to the misadventures of his befuddled secretary and sister-in-law Lucy Carter.

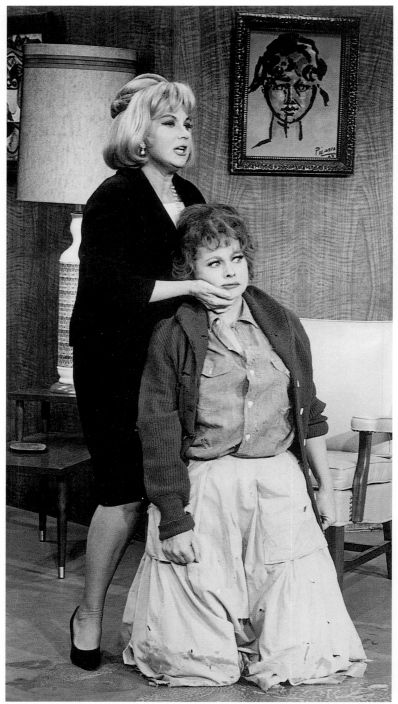

Below: After the first two seasons, guest stars such as Jack Benny, Danny Kaye, and Joan Crawford began to make appearances on the show. Lucille's old friend Ann Sothern was a frequent guest. (Note the "Picasso" of Lucy hanging on the wall.)

Above: In September 1968, Lucille brought Lucie and Desi Jr. onto the show to play Lucy's teenage kids. The show was renamed *Here's Lucy*, and Lucy Carmichael became Lucy Carter. Here, Lucie and Lucille perform a pickle dance. Lucille always checked the script to make sure that Lucie and Desi Jr. were treated equally on the show.

Right: Lucy appeared as a guest-star in the January 21, 1971 episode of Danny Thomas' series, titled *Make Room for Granddaddy*—a play on the title of Thomas' old TV series, *Make Room for Daddy*, which was filmed at Desilu.

Left: In the later years, Lucille often used guest stars to boost ratings for the show. In one of the more famous episodes, Elizabeth Taylor tries to pry her diamond wedding ring off Lucy's hand as her husband, Richard Burton, looks on. Reportedly, Burton and Taylor eventually became fed up with Lucille's tyrannical ways on the set and took a long, unscheduled coffee break to cool off.

Above, left: Lucy swoons as football star and famous playboy Joe Namath gives her a hug.

Above, right: Vincent Price tries to strangle Lucy during his guest episode.

Above: In 1966, Lucille taped a television special with Zero Mostel and Carol Burnett. Mostel said he was able to come to Hollywood from New York for the show because "my analyst was taking a vacation."

Lucille shares a tender moment with her old pal Ginger Rogers.
The two actresses had met as young women on the RKO lot
and remained fast friends ever after.

T wo queens of television comedy, guest-star Carol Burnett and
Lucy perform a song and dance number in a 1969 episode of
Here's Lucy.

Buster Keaton hands Lucy a flower during a television special on which they both appeared. A master of physical comedy, Keaton had helped Lucille hone her comedic talents in the 1940s.

THE LATER YEARS   87

Left: Lucy Carmichael, just like Lucy Ricardo, was obsessed with getting close to famous people. Here, Lucy poses as a doorman in order to meet Danny Kaye.

Below: In *Here's Lucy*, Gale Gordon played Lucy's brother-in-law and partner in an employment agency. On January 3, 1972, the venerable actress Helen Hayes appeared on the show.

Lucille first met George Burns around 1937, when she was dating Al Hall. Here, several decades later, the two comedy greats perform a vaudeville song and dance number.

Lucille's movie partner Bob Hope (center) and a stone-faced Jack Benny (left) were two of comedy's old guard who made appearances on the show. After the unpleasant taping of one episode, Jack Benny reportedly called the show's director, Herbert Kenwith, at home and said, "Herb, you must find her a psychiatrist."

ight: In 1986, at the age of
seventy-five, Lucille attemp-
ted a television sitcom
comeback with *Life with Lucy*.
Despite the high hopes of her
new network, ABC, audiences
found Lucy's shtick tired, and
the show failed. Seated from
left to right: Donovan Scott,
Larry Anderson, Jenny Lewis,
Gale Gordon, Philip J. Amelio, Jr.,
and Ann Dusenberry.

eft: Lucille played a homeless woman in the 1985 dramatic television movie *Stone Pillow*. This was a project Lucille desperately
wanted to do, but the public and critics alike responded poorly
to an un-funny portrayal, and the movie received mixed reviews.
Nonetheless, *Stone Pillow* was the eighth highest-rated program the
week it aired.

Conclusion

By 1960, the nine-year television run of Lucy and Ricky Ricardo was drawing to a close. Westinghouse's contract for *I Love Lucy* would run out after the filming of "Lucy Meets the Moustache," and neither Lucille nor Desi was interested in renewing. Their real-life marriage, unlike its television counterpart, had reached the point where the two agreed that they could neither live, nor work, together any longer.

On March 2, Desi's forty-third birthday, the cast and crew of *I Love Lucy* filed into the Desilu Playhouse to film the show's 192nd and final episode. The show co-starred television pioneer Ernie Kovacs and his wife, Edie Adams. In the show, Kovacs decides to hire Little Ricky to appear on his show instead of Ricky Sr. In classic Lucy Ricardo style, Lucy disguises herself as Kovacs' moustached chauffeur in order to try and convince him to hire her husband. The show ended with an exchange that seems ironically apropos of what the real-life couple was going through:

Lucy: "Honest, honey, I was just trying to help."

Ricky: "From now on you can help me by not trying to help me. But thanks anyway."

The two then hugged and kissed, tears running down their cheeks. As the embrace went on, Lucille said, "You're supposed to say 'cut.'" After a few more emotional moments, Desi said, "I know. Cut, goddamn it!"

Lucille Ball took the character of Lucy Ricardo, transformed her into Lucy Carmichael and eventually Lucy Carter, and continued her historic television career for many more years. But while she reigned as television's premier comedienne throughout the 1960s and much of the 1970s, her subsequent shows were never as groundbreaking nor as endearing as *I Love Lucy*. The Lucille and Desi combination possessed a special magic that neither could re-create alone.

Still, Lucille was driven by a perpetual need to make people laugh. Indeed, perhaps no other performer in the history of television has affected so many people, and elicited so much unbridled laughter, as Lucille Ball. Even today, more than twenty years after she ceased to be a regular television presence, the world's love affair with Lucille Ball continues.

Opposite: When these two legends of comedy strode onstage at the 1989 Academy Awards ceremony, they were greeted by an extended ovation. (Note Lucille's dress—she was proud to show off her still-great legs.)

Above: With a showbiz career that spanned more than fifty years; two long-running, much-loved television comedies; and more than 70 movies to her credit, Lucille Ball was an extraordinary talent—and one of the twentieth century's greatest performers.

Filmography

Bibliography

Blood Money. United Artists, 1933.

Broadway Thru a Keyhole. United Artists, 1933.

Roman Scandals. United Artists, 1933.

The Affairs of Cellini. United Artists, 1934.

Bottoms Up. Fox, 1934.

Broadway Bill. Columbia, 1934.

Bulldog Drummond Strikes Back. United Artists, 1934.

Carnival. Columbia, 1934.

The Fugitive Lady. Columbia, 1934.

Hold That Girl. Fox, 1934.

Jealousy. Columbia, 1934.

Kid Millions. United Artists, 1934.

Men of the Night. Columbia, 1934.

Moulin Rouge. United Artists, 1934.

Nana. United Artists, 1934.

I Dream Too Much. RKO, 1935.

Old Man Rhythm. RKO, 1935.

Roberta. RKO, 1935.

Top Hat. RKO, 1935.

Bunker Bean. RKO, 1936.

Chatterbox. RKO, 1936.

Follow the Fleet. RKO, 1936.

That Girl from Paris. RKO, 1936.

Don't Tell the Wife. RKO, 1937.

Stage Door. RKO, 1937.

Annabel Takes a Tour. RKO, 1938.

The Affairs of Annabel. RKO, 1938.

Go Chase Yourself. RKO, 1938.

Having a Wonderful Time. RKO, 1938.

Joy of Living. RKO, 1938.

Room Service. RKO, 1938.

The Next Time I Marry. RKO, 1938.

Beauty for the Asking. RKO, 1939.

Five Came Back. RKO, 1939.

Panama Lady. RKO, 1939.

That's Right—You're Wrong. RKO, 1939.

Twelve Crowded Hours. RKO, 1939.

Dance, Girl, Dance. RKO, 1940.

The Marines Fly High. RKO, 1940.

Too Many Girls. RKO, 1940.

You Can't Fool Your Wife. RKO, 1940.

A Girl, a Guy, and a Gob. RKO, 1941.

Look Who's Laughing. RKO, 1941.

The Big Street. RKO, 1942.

Seven Days' Leave. RKO, 1942.

Valley of the Sun. RKO, 1942.

Best Foot Forward. MGM, 1943.

DuBarry Was a Lady. MGM, 1943.

Thousands Cheer. MGM, 1943.

Meet the People. MGM, 1944.

Abbott and Costello in Hollywood. MGM, 1945.

Without Love. MGM, 1945.

The Dark Corner. Twentieth Century Fox, 1946.

Easy to Wed. MGM, 1946.

Lover Come Back. Universal, 1946.

Two Smart People. MGM, 1946.

Ziegfeld Follies. MGM, 1946.

Her Husband's Affairs. Columbia, 1947.

Lured. MGM, 1947.

Easy Living. RKO, 1949.

Miss Grant Takes Richmond. Columbia, 1949.

Sorrowful Jones. Paramount, 1949.

Fancy Pants. Paramount, 1950.

The Fuller Brush Girl. Columbia, 1950.

A Woman of Distinction. Columbia, 1950.

The Magic Carpet. Columbia, 1951.

The Long, Long Trailer. MGM, 1954.

Forever Darling. MGM, 1956.

The Facts of Life. United Artists, 1960.

Critic's Choice. Warner Brothers, 1963.

A Guide for the Married Man. Twentieth Century Fox, 1967.

Yours, Mine and Ours. United Artists, 1968.

Mame. Warner Brothers, 1974.

Andrews, Bart. *The "I Love Lucy" Book*. New York: Doubleday, 1985.

Brady, Kathleen. *Lucille: The Life of Lucille Ball*. New York: Hyperion, 1994.

Brochu, Jim. *Lucy in the Afternoon*. New York: William Morrow, 1990.

Hay, Peter. *MGM: When the Lion Roars*. Atlanta: Turner Publishing, 1991.

Katz, Ephraim. *The Film Encyclopedia*. New York: Putnam.

Lucille Ball: First Lady of Comedy. New York: Museum of Broadcasting, 1984.

McClay, Michael, and Deanna Gaffner-McClay. *I Love Lucy: The Complete Picture History of the Most Popular TV Show Ever*. New York: Warner Books, 1995.

Sanders, Coyne Steven, and Tom Gilbert. *Desilu: The Story of Lucille Ball and Desi Arnaz*. New York: Quill, 1994.

Wyman, Ric B. *For the Love of Lucy: The Complete Guide for Collectors and Fans*. New York: Abbeyville Press, 1995

Index